California

by Jason Glaser

Consultant:
Melinda A. Peak
Senior Historian
Peak & Associates, Inc.

Capstone press
Mankato, Minnesota

Capstone Press
151 Good Counsel Drive • P.O. Box 669 • Mankato, Minnesota 56002
http://www.capstone-press.com

Library of Congress Cataloging-in-Publication Data
Glaser, Jason.
    California / by Jason Glaser.
    v. cm.—(Land of liberty)
    Includes bibliographical references and index.
    Contents: About California—Land, climate, and wildlife—History of
California—Government and politics—Economy and resources—People and
culture—Timeline—State seal and flag.
    ISBN 0-7368-1573-2 (hardcover)
    1. California—Juvenile literature. [1. California.] I. Title. II. Series.
F861.3 .G58 2003
979.4—dc21   2002010319

Summary: An introduction to the geography, history, government, politics,
    economy, resources, people, and culture of California, including maps, charts,
    and a recipe.

Editorial Credits
Bradley P. Hoehn and Christopher Harbo, editors; Eric Kudalis, product planning
    editor; Jennifer Schonborn, series and book designer; Angi Gahler, illustrator;
    Kelly Garvin, photo researcher

Photo Credits
Cover images: Golden Gate Bridge, San Francisco, Digital Stock; zinfandel grapes
    on the vine, Craig Lovell

Capstone Press/Gary Sundermeyer, 54; Corbis, 27, 28–29, 57; Corbis/AFP, 53;
Corbis/Bettmann, 26; Corbis/David Butow, 34; Corbis/Chris Daniels, 36;
Corbis/Charles O'Rear, 38–39; Corbis/Roger Ressmeyer 17, 41; Corbis/Phil
Schermeister, 44; Corbis/Wally McNamee, 35; Courtesy of the California History
Room, California State Library, Sacramento, California, 24; Digital Stock, 1, 56;
Houserstock/Dave G. Houser, 21, 43, 63; Houserstock/Ellen Barone, 30;
Houserstock/Jan Butchofsky, 4, 8, 48, 50–51, 52; Hulton Archive by Getty
Images, 18, 22, 58; Lissa Funk, 14–15; One Mile Up, Inc, 55 (both);
Tom Till, 42; U.S. Postal Service, 59; Will Funk, 12, 13

Artistic Effects
Digital Stock, PhotoDisc, Inc.

1 2 3 4 5 6 08 07 06 05 04 03

Table of Contents

People make Rose Parade floats
with thousands of real flowers.

Chapter 1

About California

For more than 100 years, people have gathered on New Year's Day to watch the Tournament of Roses Parade. This parade in Pasadena, California, was first held in 1890. People rode through Pasadena in horse-drawn carriages covered in roses and other flowers. The tournament was created to bring attention to California's beautiful scenery and climate.

Today, the Tournament of Roses parade is called the Rose Parade. More than 1 million people come out to watch the parade each year. Every year, a college football game called the Rose Bowl is played after the Rose Parade.

The Rose Parade travels 5.5 miles (8.9 kilometers) and is filled with marching bands, horse troops, and giant floats. In

2002, the floats were covered with more than 40 million blossoms. Float designers begin creating the next year's floats as soon as the Rose Parade is over.

The Golden State

California has often been thought of as a land of opportunity. Its nickname is the Golden State because of its long history with gold. In the mid-1800s, thousands of people moved to California in hopes of striking it rich in the gold fields. Today, many people travel to the state to enjoy its warm climate and rich culture.

California is located along the West Coast of the United States. California is bordered by the states of Oregon, Nevada, and Arizona. Mexico borders California on the south. California has an area of 163,707 square miles (424,001 square kilometers). Of the states, only Alaska and Texas are larger in land area.

California is an important part of the United States. Millions of Americans use the products that come from California. The state contributes billions of dollars to the nation's economy.

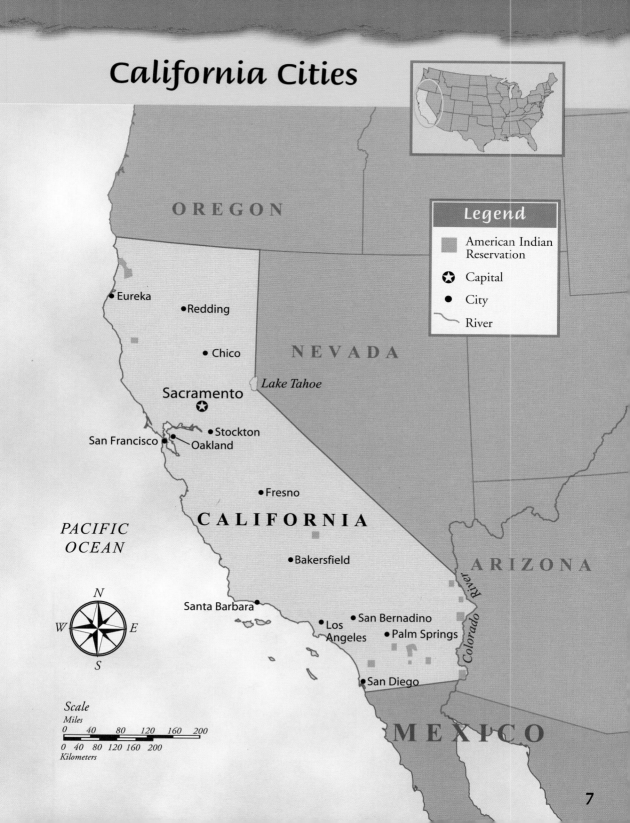

California Cities

OREGON

NEVADA

Legend
- American Indian Reservation
- ★ Capital
- ● City
- ～ River

- Eureka
- Redding
- Chico
- Sacramento ★
- Lake Tahoe
- Stockton
- San Francisco
- Oakland
- Fresno

CALIFORNIA

PACIFIC OCEAN

- Bakersfield
- Santa Barbara
- Los Angeles
- San Bernadino
- Palm Springs
- San Diego

ARIZONA

Colorado River

MEXICO

N
W E
S

Scale
Miles
0 40 80 120 160 200
0 40 80 120 160 200
Kilometers

7

California's Big Sur region is a 90-mile (145-kilometer) stretch of scenic coastline between San Francisco and Los Angeles.

Chapter 2

Land, Climate, and Wildlife

California is the third largest state in the United States. The coastline of California stretches 1,264 miles (2,034 kilometers) from Oregon to Mexico.

In the mainland United States, California holds the highest and lowest points. Mount Whitney in central California is 14,495 feet (4,418 meters) high. Badwater Basin in Death Valley is 282 feet (86 meters) below sea level. Mount Whitney and Badwater Basin are only 80 miles (129 kilometers) apart.

California is a state with many land features. Coastlands and islands form California's western border. Mountains, valleys, and deserts fill out the rest of this long, narrow state.

"Variety is king. That's the way it is in California."
—Zov Karamardian, restaurant owner and
famous chef, Tustin, California

Coastlands

The coastline of California borders the Pacific Ocean. The coastline runs south and east in a diagonal direction. California's coast moves so far east that Los Angeles is farther east than Reno in the neighboring state of Nevada.

California's coast has many shipping harbors. San Diego, San Francisco, and Eureka have natural harbors. The ship harbor in Los Angeles was made by workers. They cut into the land to make a waterway to the city.

More than half of California's people live near the coastline. Most of them live in the harbor cities of San Diego, San Francisco, and Los Angeles.

Pounding waves push tiny animals and plants called plankton to California's coast. Many animals feed on plankton. Sea otters, elephant seals, and other ocean mammals live near California's southern coastline. Each day, thousands of birds feed and nest on the coast.

California's Land Features

Redwood National Park

Klamath River

CASCADE RANGE

Pit River

Lassen Volcanic National Park

Sacramento River

PACIFIC OCEAN

Russian River

CENTRAL VALLEY

SIERRA NEVADA

Lake Tahoe

San Francisco Harbor

Yosemite National Park

Mono Lake

COAST RANGES

Kings Canyon National Park

Mount Whitney

Salinas River

Sequoia National Park

Kern River

Death Valley National Park

MOJAVE DESERT

Channel Islands National Park

Mojave River

Joshua Tree National Park

Colorado River

SONORAN DESERT

N
W E
S

Scale
Miles
0   40   80   120   160
0   40   80   120   160
Kilometers

Legend

- - - California Aqueduct
- · - Colorado River Aqueduct
▲ Highest Point
- - - Los Angeles Aqueduct
⛰ Mountain Range
▪ National Park
〰 River

Sequoias

Sequoia trees grow in the Sierra Nevada range. Sequoias are not as tall as coastal redwoods, but many are bigger around. The largest living thing in the world is a sequoia called General Sherman. Its trunk is more than 102 feet (31 meters) around at its base. Scientists believe General Sherman's trunk weighs about 1,385 tons (1,256 metric tons).

Forests cover California's northern coastline. Redwoods grow in northern California. Redwoods are the tallest trees in the world. The tallest tree is the Mendocino redwood tree. It rises to 367 feet, 6 inches (112 meters) in the Montgomery Woods State Reserve.

Mountains

Long ago, volcanoes and earthquakes created mountains in California. The Cascades are California's northernmost mountains. Some of these mountains are actually volcanoes. The Klamath Mountains also are found in the north. Western California is home to the Coast Ranges. A mountain range called the Sierra Nevada lies along California's border with Nevada. The Sierra Nevada range has the tallest mountains in the 48-state area.

California's few natural lakes are found mostly in mountain areas. Lake Tahoe is the largest mountain lake in North America. The lake's water is so clear that people can see 69 feet (21 meters) deep.

The Sierra Nevada range lies along much of California's eastern border.

Central Valley

Between the western coast and the eastern mountains, the land flattens to a valley. Cows, sheep, and other animals graze on the flat, grassy land.

The Central Valley region is good for farming, even though some areas receive little rain. Mountain streams controlled by dams bring needed moisture. Valley farmers grow apples, peaches, pears, and apricots. Farmers also grow almonds, pecans, walnuts, and pistachios in the valley. Grape growers use their crops to make California's wine and raisins.

Deserts

Little plant life grows in California's deserts because of the area's small amounts of rainfall. Less than 5 inches (13 centimeters) of rain falls in most desert areas each year. Cacti and shrubs grow thick leaves and skins to help them hold water.

The Mojave (mo-HAH-vay) Desert stretches south from the southern edge of the Sierra Nevada to the Colorado Desert and east into Nevada and Utah. A common plant in

Joshua Tree National Park is located in California's Mojave Desert. Joshua tree forests grow in the park.

the Mojave is the Joshua tree. Many people visit the desert's Joshua Tree National Park every year.

California, Arizona, and Mexico share the Sonoran Desert. It is farther south than the Mojave and closer to sea level. The saguaro (sah-WAR-oh) cactus is common in the Sonoran.

Many desert animals have adapted to life in California's deserts. They sleep during the hot days and are active at night when temperatures are cooler. Bighorn sheep, deer, and coyotes are a few of the desert animals.

Environmental Issues

Earthquakes present the biggest threat of natural disaster in California. California spreads across two large pieces of Earth's crust called plates. These plates move and push against each other. They move a few inches each year. The area where the two plates meet is called a fault. The San Andreas fault stretches from the California-Mexico border north to San Francisco. When one of the plates slides, an earthquake occurs along the

In 1989, an earthquake in San Francisco damaged many buildings, cars, and roads. The earthquake killed 67 people and injured more than 3,000.

fault. Large earthquakes can destroy buildings, roads, and bridges and sometimes damage whole cities.

Pollution is another danger to Californians. Chemicals from cars, factories, and other sources mix with the air to create smog. Smog looks like gray fog or clouds of smoke. Over time, breathing smog can cause lung problems. Californians look for ways to reduce smog. Some drive electric cars, while others increase their use of public transportation.

Francis Drake arrived in California in 1579. He claimed part of California for England.

Chapter 3

History of California

American Indians have lived in California for thousands of years. The Ohlone people lived along the central California coast long before European explorers arrived.

In 1542, Juan Rodríguez Cabrillo sailed from Mexico to southern California. His crew was looking for a way around or through California, but they did not find it. Cabrillo explored near the area that is now Santa Barbara.

English explorers also came to California. In 1579, Francis Drake reached California. Drake named an area Nova Albion and declared it the property of England. Today, the area is known as Marin County.

Did you know...?
In 1510, a Spanish writer named Garci Rodríguez Ordóñez de Montalvo wrote a book called *Las Sergas de Esplandián*. He described a land called California. When Spanish explorers came to North America, they thought they had found the land described in the book. These explorers may have given California its name.

The Missions

Spain sent a teacher and missionary named Junípero Serra to California. He wanted to bring the Roman Catholic religion to as many American Indians as he could. In 1769, Serra built the first California mission. This church was called San Diego de Alcalá. He later built eight more missions in California. Other Christian missionaries built 13 missions stretching from San Diego to north of San Francisco.

Missionaries brought American Indians to live in the missions. They were baptized and taught to farm and build. Indians who tried to escape were captured and brought back to the mission. The Ohlone were not allowed to speak their own language or practice their own religion. Missionaries wanted the natives to build and live in new Spanish-style towns and cities.

About 10,000 Ohlone were living in California before the Spanish arrived. Forty years later, only about 2,000 Ohlone

Mission San Diego de Alcalá was the first of California's 21 Spanish missions.

were left. Many of the Ohlone who lived at the missions became sick or died. Europeans carried smallpox, measles, and other diseases that the Ohlones' bodies could not fight. Those who survived worked and farmed almost like slaves.

Since the Ohlone could put up little resistance, the Spanish claimed the area. They called it New Spain. Many settlers from Spain and other areas settled in New Spain.

California Changes Hands

In 1821, the people of New Spain declared independence from Spain. They called this new country Mexico. Mexico began trading with the United States. American trappers and settlers came west to live and work within Mexico.

In 1846, John Frémont led a group of American soldiers into California. The Mexican government asked the soldiers to leave. Instead, the soldiers raised the American flag above their camp and built a fort. Tensions between Mexico and the United States grew. On May 13, 1846, war broke out between the two countries.

John Frémont first began exploring California in 1843. He returned to California in 1846.

News of the Mexican War (1846-1848) did not reach all of the people living in California right away. In June 1846, a group of Americans took over the Mexican headquarters at Sonoma. They raised a flag declaring independence from Mexico. The flag showed a bear, a lone star, and the words "California Republic." Because of this flag, people called the event the Bear Flag Revolt. By 1848, Mexico surrendered its claim to the land. California became part of the United States.

Gold Rush

On January 24, 1848, a lumber worker named James Marshall found gold at Sutter's Mill in northern California. News of the discovery spread quickly. Within a year, people from all over the country came to California looking for gold.

The gold rush caused California's population to grow. Americans and immigrants from other countries moved to California. Few people found gold. Most people had to find a new way to live. Some of them set up businesses and shops.

The gold rush caused some problems in California. Robbery and other crimes were common in parts of the state. The people in California decided it was time to create a state government. California applied for statehood. In 1850, California was admitted into the Union as a state.

Westward Expansion

Even after the gold rush ended, California was a land of opportunity. People could buy large areas of land for little money. Farmers had the chance to own large farms. More people and more farms created many new jobs in California.

In the 1850s, thousands of men and some women searched for gold in rivers and streams at the base of the Sierra Nevada mountain range.

The demand for more land had a price. Some American Indians were forced onto reservations. These lands are set aside for use by American Indians. The first reservations in California were set up in 1853.

Did you know...?
The original treaties between American Indians and the federal government promised 8.5 million acres (3.4 million hectares) of California land. But less than 500,000 acres (202,000 hectares) were actually given to the American Indians.

By 1860, the United States' increasing demand for fruit made fruit growing popular in California. Farmers began growing different types of oranges. Wine makers from France and Italy planted grape vines they had brought from Europe.

Not even the destructive 1906 San Francisco earthquake or the beginning of World War I (1914–1918) slowed California's growth. Manufacturing plants made products that were used for wartime efforts.

Hard Times

In the 1930s, California was a symbol of hope to many people. The United States was in the middle of the Great Depression (1929–1939). People had invested money in the stock market and lost most or all of it when the market crashed. Others lost crops because of drought. Many people traveled west in hopes of sharing in the wealth of California.

When these travelers reached California, not enough jobs were available. People tried to survive by working in the fields and orchards. Many people lived in rundown houses and did not have enough food and clothing.

On December 7, 1941, Japan attacked Pearl Harbor. The United States then entered World War II (1939–1945). Japanese people had been living in the United States for many

Many families who moved to California during the Great Depression lived in squatters camps. Doctors sometimes visited the camps to give children shots to prevent diseases.

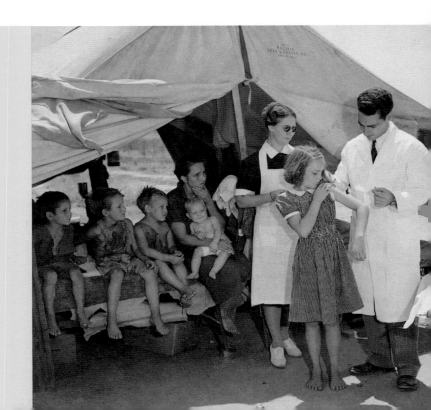

A police officer searches the bags of Japanese Americans as they arrive at a Los Angeles internment camp in 1942.

years. Many people began to believe Japanese and Japanese Americans in California could be spies. Japanese people living in California were forced out of their homes and into camps. Their farmlands, homes, and businesses were taken away or sold. They were released from the camps when the war ended in 1945.

Continuing to Grow

Californians built many ships, guns, airplanes, and supplies for the war effort. In Hollywood, movie studios made movies to raise the spirits of U.S. citizens. California's war efforts helped its economic future. Farmers continued to grow oranges, lemons, grapes, and other fruits.

After the war, technology became an important business in California. The aerospace business produced airplanes and

rockets. Companies like Hewlett-Packard created computers that helped make technology available to more people.

Today, California is also home to many software companies. Software companies make programs for computers, video games, industrial machines, and technology used to make robots. Some companies, such as Industrial Light and Magic (ILM), create software for the movie business. ILM is famous for creating special effects in movies.

During World War II, many women worked in California's airplane factories. These women are working on the noses of bomber airplanes.

The California State Capitol is called a "working museum." Visitors tour the building to learn about California's past, while lawmakers pass laws that shape the state's future.

Chapter 4

Government and Politics

California's large population gives the state power in national politics. All states elect two members to the U.S. Senate. Each state elects members to the House of Representatives based on its population. California has 52 representatives. California's 52 representatives and two senators gives the state 54 electoral votes.

California has more electoral votes than any other state. Electoral votes are cast during presidential elections. Candidates receive all the electoral votes from states where they earn a majority of the popular vote. California does not always vote for the same political party from election to

election. Presidential candidates from all parties work hard to encourage Californians to vote for them.

Branches of Government

California's state government is made up of three branches. The governor leads the executive branch. California elects its governors to four-year terms. The state senate and state assembly are the legislative branch. The two houses of the legislature write and pass California's laws. California's judicial branch is led by the state supreme court. The courts of appeal and superior courts are also part of California's judicial branch.

California and Political Issues

California's state legislature makes most of the laws that govern the state. In 1911, political reform gave Californians the power to sponsor their own laws. Ideas that have enough support become ballot propositions. Californians then vote to see if the propositions will become law. Californians have passed

California's State Government

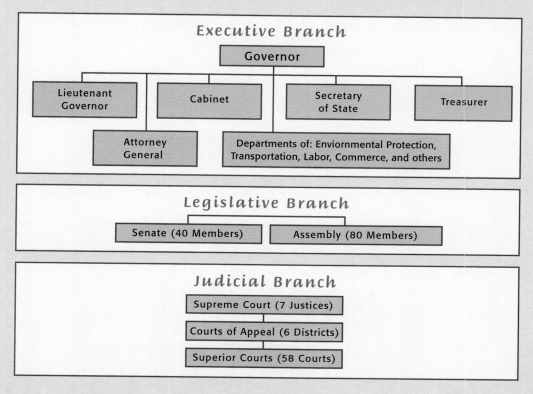

Executive Branch

Governor

Lieutenant Governor | Cabinet | Secretary of State | Treasurer

Attorney General | Departments of: Enviornmental Protection, Transportation, Labor, Commerce, and others

Legislative Branch

Senate (40 Members) | Assembly (80 Members)

Judicial Branch

Supreme Court (7 Justices)

Courts of Appeal (6 Districts)

Superior Courts (58 Courts)

propositions to make drinking water cleaner and to lower property taxes.

Crime rates in California are similar to those in other highly populated states. But crime is often a problem in larger California cities. Large gangs operate in cities like Los Angeles and Oakland. Gangs control their neighborhoods by using violence and threats.

Education is an important issue in California. The state's large population causes a great need for good teachers. Because California shares a border with Mexico, many Spanish-speaking children attend California schools. Schools need teachers who speak English and Spanish. The demand for teachers, schools, and materials is costly. Funding educational needs in California is often a challenge.

Some California schools hold classes year-round. These elementary students attend class in July.

Dianne Feinstein

Dianne Feinstein was born in San Francisco, California. She became a member of the California women's parole board when she was 27. The parole board decides if prisoners in California jails qualify for an early release from prison.

From 1969 to 1978, Feinstein served on the San Francisco Board of Supervisors. In 1978, Feinstein became mayor of San Francisco after the former mayor died. She was elected mayor in 1979 and again in 1981. As mayor, Feinstein focused on reducing crime to make the San Francisco area safer. Feinstein helped create more jobs and a stronger economy.

In 1992, Feinstein was elected to the U.S. Senate after another California senator resigned. She was reelected in 1994 and 2000. She is the first woman to serve on the Senate Judiciary Committee. This committee makes laws on civil liberties and constitutional amendments.

Large cranes load California's goods onto cargo ships. California ships its goods to many countries around the world.

Chapter 5

Economy and Resources

California's economy is larger than all but four countries in the world. In 2001, California's gross state product grew to more than $1.5 trillion. Gross state product is the value of all the goods and services produced in a state.

Workers in California earn higher average wages than workers in other parts of the United States. California also has a higher cost of living, which means living expenses are higher there than in other states.

California has a strong relationship with nearby countries. More than one-fourth of California's goods are exported to Mexico. Canada and many Asian countries also buy goods from California.

Agriculture

Agriculture is a major part of California's economy. The state
is the leading producer of agricultural goods in the United
States. Texas is second and Iowa is third. In 2000, California's
total agricultural sales were more than those of Texas and
Iowa combined.

Grapes are one of California's most important crops. The
Sonoma and Napa Valley grape vineyards are famous for the
wine they produce. Farmers there also raise almonds, cotton,
and many vegetables. Much of the food Americans eat comes

from California. The state's raisins, avocados, olives, and prunes are some foods often found in American stores.

California has more dairy cattle than any other state. After grapes, milk is California's second biggest agricultural product.

Energy and Natural Resources

The United States depends on many other countries for oil and petroleum. Oil and petroleum products include gas and plastics. Unlike most of the United States, California drills

California's Napa Valley is famous for its vineyards. Workers pick grapes by hand. The grapes are taken to a winery to be pressed and made into wine.

some of its own oil. Southeastern California has most of California's oil wells. California's oil refineries make nearly two million barrels of petroleum products per day.

Mining is an important part of California's economy. California is the third largest gold producer, behind Utah and Nevada. The state also produces iron, copper, salt, silver, and talc. California is the only place in the United States that mines and processes boron and asbestos. Boron is used to make household cleaners. Asbestos is used to make cement and brake linings. California also exports about 14 million tons (13 million metric tons) of sand and gravel.

Manufacturing

Aerospace technology once was one of California's largest industries. California aerospace plants helped create many types of aircraft. Boeing and Lockheed are airplane manufacturers based in California. Engineers in California also developed the space shuttle design that is still in use today. The aerospace industry decreased in the 1990s. Still,

California's oil refineries turn crude oil into gasoline, jet fuel, and other petroleum products.

more than 1,000 companies in California make more than $28 billion in aerospace materials each year.

The Silicon Valley is an area in northern California with many technology companies. Silicon is a metal that is used to make computer chips. Businesses in Silicon Valley make computers, monitors, security devices, and video games. Apple Computer designs hardware and software for computers. Intel

41

and Sun Microsystems are among the other California businesses that make computers.

Service and Tourism

Tourism and other service industries make up California's largest source of revenue. More Americans visit California than any other state. In 1998, visitors in California spent more than $67 billion in the state.

Many popular tourist spots are found in southern California. Disneyland, Sea World, and the San Diego Zoo

Yosemite Falls is one of the many sites to see in Yosemite National Park.

Orcas, also known as killer whales, put on shows for visitors at
Sea World in San Diego.

are just a few. In northern California, people can visit Alcatraz
Island, Yosemite National Park, and the wine country.

One of California's most popular services is the movie
industry. Most of the major motion picture studios in the
United States are located in California. Universal Studios and
Warner Brothers Studios attract millions of visitors each year.

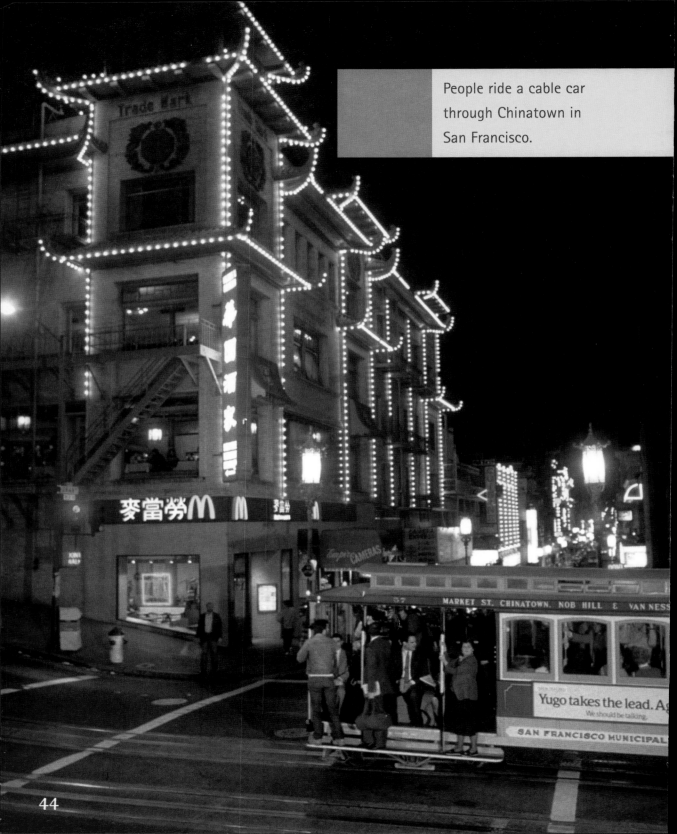

People ride a cable car through Chinatown in San Francisco.

Chapter 6

People and Culture

California has a diverse population. Together, California's minority groups make up the largest minority population of any other state. One-third of the people in California are Hispanic. Large numbers of Mexicans have been coming to California during the last 50 years. Other Hispanic groups include immigrants from Central America and South America.

Asians are the third largest group in California, behind white and Hispanic. Since the late 1800s, Chinese, Japanese, Korean, and other Asian workers have settled in California. In

1870, Chinese workers were 20 percent of the state's labor force. Today, nearly 4 million Asians live in California.

California's diverse population is an important part of the state's culture, but race relations in the state have not always been smooth. While most Californians respect the differences between races, racial tension has sometimes led to violence. The Watts riots in 1965 and the Rodney King riots in 1991 were both a result of violence against African Americans.

Today, California is working hard to improve race relations. The state promotes African American studies and cultural awareness in the United States.

Language

A person in California is likely to hear more than one language on any given day. Most people in California speak English. Many speak Spanish as either their first language or second language. California schools provide bilingual

California's Ethnic Background

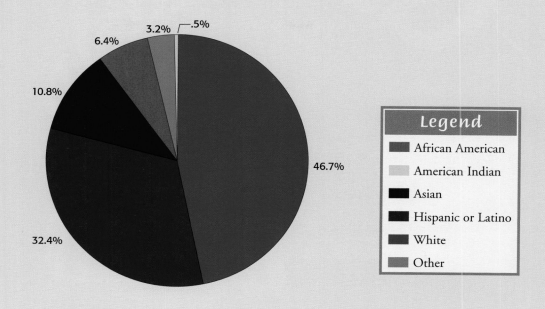

Legend	
	African American
	American Indian
	Asian
	Hispanic or Latino
	White
	Other

46.7%

32.4%

10.8%

6.4%

3.2%

.5%

education. Many government and legal forms are available in both English and Spanish.

Food

The differences among people in California show in the cooking styles across the state. Southern California restaurants have many dishes that include spicy barbecue and Mexican

The Ghirardelli Chocolate Company began making chocolate in San Francisco in 1852.

food. Sushi bars are very popular in coastal cities and areas where Asian people live. Sushi is a type of food made with raw fish, rice, and vinegar.

California is also known for its healthy lifestyles. Many Californians eat seafood. Salmon is a popular fish in the state's restaurants. Californian recipes tend to favor natural plants, herbs, and spices. Locally grown crops provide fresh fruits and vegetables, nuts, rice, and other healthy foods.

Californians also have a history of eating chocolate. Explorers who visited the areas of California, Mexico, and South America brought cocoa beans back to Europe. Cocoa beans are used to make chocolate. Miners bought and sold chocolate during the gold rush.

People and Transportation

Most people in California live in urban areas, such as Los Angeles and San Francisco. Homes in California are expensive. Many people live in apartments or condominiums. In the largest areas of California, people often have to travel long distances in heavy traffic to get to work. Traveling from one side of Los Angeles to another can take as long as two hours.

Californians use many types of transportation. People in California own more than 22 million cars. California uses more gas per year than most countries. People in California also use trains, subways, buses, boats, and other forms of mass transit. These systems help reduce traffic and gasoline use.

California Fun

Millions of tourists come to California each year. Many people travel to Hollywood to see where their favorite TV shows or movies were filmed. Beaches are popular during the winter when it is colder in many parts of the United States.

Theme parks like Universal Studios and Legoland provide enjoyable vacations for children and adults.

California has many art museums. Some museums display works from African American artists and Mexican artists. One of the world's most famous art museums is in California. In 1953, the wealthy businessman J. Paul Getty opened the J. Paul Getty Museum in his Malibu home. After Getty died, the museum's trustees made plans for a larger and better location. In 1997, the Getty Center opened in Los Angeles.

Visitors to Legoland in southern California can see miniature cities made completely from Legos.

Olympics

Los Angeles hosted the Olympic Games in 1932 and again in 1984. The 23rd Summer Olympiad in 1984 was one of the most watched Olympic Games in American history. The United States won 174 medals that year.

People in California enjoy many styles of music. Classical composer Igor Stravinsky worked and lived in California. Other California composers write musical scores for Hollywood movies. Leo Fender was an inventor who lived in California in the 1940s. His Fender guitars are popular with rock and roll musicians. Musicians from California have influenced jazz, soul music, and modern rap. Jazz festivals are held each year in many California cities. The Beach Boys and the Grateful Dead also helped shape the sound of California rock music.

Many California cities are represented in professional sports. California has five pro baseball teams, three pro football teams, and three pro hockey teams. The state also has four men's pro basketball teams and two women's pro basketball teams.

Each year, millions of people visit California. They enjoy the Golden State's history, cultural diversity, and scenery. Spanish missions, San Francisco's Chinatown, and Yosemite National Park are just a few of the state's attractions. California is one of the few places in the nation where people can go to the beach, the desert, and the mountains all in one day.

The San Diego Padres and the San Francisco Giants are two of California's five pro baseball teams. The Padres and Giants play each other many times during the regular season.

Recipe: Raisin Snickerdoodles

California is one of the world's largest producers of raisins. Raisin snickerdoodles are a fun and delicious way to enjoy one of California's most important crops.

Ingredients

2 tablespoons (30 mL) sugar
2 teaspoons (10 mL) cinnamon
1 cup (240 mL) butter or
    margarine, softened
1½ cups (360 mL) sugar
2 eggs
2¾ cups (655 mL) all-purpose
    flour
1½ teaspoons (7.5 mL) cream of
    tartar
1 teaspoon (5 mL) baking soda
¼ teaspoon (1.2 mL) salt
1½ cups (360 mL) raisins

Equipment

non-stick cooking spray
baking sheets
mixing bowls (3)
mixing spoons
measuring spoons
dry-ingredient measuring cups
oven mitts
spatula
wire cooling racks

What You Do

1. Heat oven to 375°F (190°C).

2. Spray baking sheets with non-stick cooking spray. Set aside.

3. In a bowl, mix sugar with cinnamon to make cinnamon sugar. Set aside.

4. Combine butter and sugar into second bowl. Beat with spoon until mixture is light and fluffy.

5. Crack eggs and add to butter mixture. Stir well.

6. Combine flour, cream of tartar, baking soda and salt in a third bowl. Add to butter mixture and mix well. Stir in raisins.

7. Shape dough into 1-inch (2.5-centimeter) balls with your hands. Roll balls in cinnamon sugar mixture until well coated.

8. Place sugared balls 2 inches (5 centimeters) apart on prepared baking sheets.

9. Bake on top rack of oven for 10 to 12 minutes or until cookies are golden brown around the edges.

10. Remove baking sheets with oven mitts. Let cool 1 minute.

11. Remove cookies from baking sheets with spatula.

12. Cool cookies on wire racks.

Makes 3½ dozen cookies

California's Flag and Seal

California's Flag

California's state flag was adopted by the California Legislature in 1911. The flag is based on the Bear Flag that a group of Americans raised over Sonoma in 1846. The bear represents the many grizzly bears that once lived in California. The star is based on the lone star of Texas.

California's State Seal

California's state seal was adopted by the Constitutional Convention of 1849. The woman on the seal is Minerva, the Roman goddess of wisdom. The grizzly bear at her feet symbolizes California's wildlife. The miner in the distance stands for California's gold mining history. The word "Eureka" stands for the discovery of gold. The word means "I found it" in Greek.

Almanac

Nickname: Golden State

Population: 33,871,648 (U.S. Census 2000)
Population rank: 1st

Capital: Sacramento

Largest cities: Los Angeles, San Diego, San Jose, San Francisco, Long Beach

Agricultural products: Vegetables, fruits and nuts, dairy products, cattle, grapes

Average summer temperature: 73 degrees Fahrenheit (23 degrees Celsius)

Average winter temperature: 46 degrees Fahrenheit (8 degrees Celsius)

Average annual precipitation: 22 inches (56 centimeters)

Area: 163,707 square miles (424,001 square kilometers)
Size rank: 3rd

Highest point: Mount Whitney, 14,495 feet (4,418 meters) above sea level

Lowest point: Badwater Basin (Death Valley) 282 feet (86 meters) below sea level

Grizzly bear

Golden Poppy

Economy

Natural resources: Asbestos, borax, bromine, copper, gold, iron ore, marble, platinum, silver

Types of industry: Electronic equipment, aerospace equipment, film production, food processing, petroleum, computers, tourism

Symbols

Animal: Grizzly bear

Bird: California valley quail

Dance: West Coast swing dancing

Fish: Golden trout

Flower: Golden poppy

Symbols

Gem: Benitoite

Mineral: Gold

Reptile: Desert tortoise

Rock: Serpentine

Song: "I Love You, California" by F. B. Silverwood

Tree: California redwood

Government

First governor: Peter H. Burnett

Statehood: September 9, 1850 (31st state)

U.S. Representatives: 52

U.S. Senators: 2

U.S. electoral votes: 54

Counties: 58

Timeline

State History

1542
Juan Rodríguez Cabrillo arrives in Southern California.

1579
Francis Drake arrives in California.

1769
First Spanish mission is built in California.

1821
Mexico declares independence from Spain.

1848
Gold is discovered at Sutter's Mill; Mexico gives California to the United States.

1850
California is admitted as the 31st state.

U.S. History

1620
Pilgrims establish a colony in the New World.

1775–1783
American colonists fight for their freedom from Great Britain in the Revolutionary War.

1812–1814
The United States and Great Britain fight the War of 1812.

1846–1848
The United States and Mexico fight the Mexican War.

1861–1865
The Civil War is fought.

1930s
Thousands of people move to California looking for jobs during the Great Depression.

1942
Japanese Americans are sent to internment camps during World War II.

1991
Los Angeles experiences six days of riots after the Rodney King trial.

1906
Huge earthquake destroys much of San Francisco.

1984
Los Angeles hosts the summer Olympics.

2001
California experiences an energy crisis.

1929–1939
The United States experiences the Great Depression.

1964
U.S. Congress passes the Civil Rights Act which makes discrimination illegal.

1914–1918
World War I is fought; the United States enters the war in 1917.

1939–1945
World War II is fought; the United States enters the war in 1941.

2001
On September 11, terrorists attack the World Trade Center and the Pentagon.

59

Words to Know

aerospace (AIR-oh-spayss)—relating to the science of jet flight and space travel

bilingual (bye-LING-gwuhl)—able to speak two languages

diverse (duh-VURSS)—to be varied or assorted; a diverse population is made up of people of different races or cultures.

drought (DROUT)—a long period of time with little or no rainfall

internment camp (in-TURN-muhnt KAMP)—a camp set up by the U.S. government during World War II to hold people of Japanese descent

mass transit (MASS TRAN-sit)—a system of trains, subways, or buses that carry people in large numbers

mission (MISH-uhn)—a church or place that is built to teach people about Christian religions

pollution (puh-LOO-shuhn)—harmful materials that damage the environment

riot (RYE-uht)—a group of people acting noisy, violent, and out of control

smog (SMOG)—a mixture of fog and smoke that hangs in the air over large cities

To Learn More

Altman, Linda Jacobs. *California.* Celebrate the States. New York: Benchmark Books, 1997.

Green, Carl R. *The California Trail to Gold in American History.* In American History. Berkeley Heights, N.J.: Enslow, 2000.

Kennedy, Teresa. *California.* From Sea to Shining Sea. New York: Children's Press, 2001.

Monroe, Judy. *The California Gold Rush.* Let Freedom Ring. Mankato, Minn.: Bridgestone Books, 2002.

Internet Sites

Track down many sites about California.
Visit the FACT HOUND at *http://www.facthound.com*

IT IS EASY! IT IS FUN!
1) Go to *http://www.facthound.com*
2) Type in: 0736815732
3) Click on "FETCH IT" and
   FACT HOUND will find several
   links hand-picked by our editors.

Relax and let our pal FACT HOUND do the research for you!

Places to Write and Visit

California Historical Society
678 Mission Street
San Francisco, CA 94105

California Space Institute
University of California at San Diego
9500 Gilman Drive
La Jolla, CA 92093

The Getty Center
1200 Getty Center Drive
Los Angeles, CA 90049-1679

Museum of the City of San Francisco
PMB 423
945 Taraval Street
San Francisco, CA 94116

Wind farms use large windmills, called turbines, to create some of California's electricity.

Index